T0266338

# Enriching Our Worship 1

## Morning and Evening Prayer
## The Great Litany
## The Holy Eucharist

*Supplemental Liturgical Materials prepared by*
*The Standing Liturgical Commission 1997*

 CHURCH

CHURCH PUBLISHING INCORPORATED, NEW YORK

Copyright © 1998 by The Church Pension Fund

Portions of this book may be reproduced by a congregation for its own use. Commercial or large-scale reproduction, or reproduction for sale, of any portion of this book or of the book as a whole, without the written permission of Church Publishing Incorporated, is prohibited.

Church Publishing Incorporated
445 Fifth Avenue
New York, NY 10016

ISBN-13 978-0-89869-275-4

**11**

# Contents

# Preface
*by*
*The Most Reverend Frank Tracy Griswold*

*Enriching Our Worship* is offered by the Standing Liturgical Commission to the Church through the General Convention as an enrichment of our liturgical prayer. This collection is part of an ongoing process of listening to what the Spirit is saying to the Church through the diverse experience of those who gather to worship and to celebrate the sacramental rites which fashion and identify us as the People of God.

*Enriching Our Worship* is not intended to supplant the Book of Common Prayer, but rather to provide additional resources to assist worshiping communities wishing to expand the language, images and metaphors used in worship. In some cases the canticles and prayers represent the recovery of ancient biblical and patristic images, such as the identification of Christ with Wisdom, and in other cases images which speak of God in other than the familiar masculine terms which have been so much a part of our liturgical prayer. Expanding our vocabulary of prayer and the ways in which we name the Holy One bear witness to the fact that the mystery of God transcends all categories of knowing, including those of masculine and feminine.

One of the considerations in choosing or developing the texts included in this collection has been the prayer experience of women, and the desire to honor that experience while remaining faithful to the constituent elements and norms of liturgical prayer as this Church has received and understood them. At all points along the way in the process of selection and development of texts the question has been asked: Is this text consistent with the

Trinitarian and Christological formulations which we, as Anglicans, regard as normative and the ground of our common prayer?

The local use of *Enriching Our Worship* is subject to authorization by the Bishop, who serves as the Chief Liturgical Minister of the Diocese. In this way a pastoral bond can be maintained which relates the local use of these texts to the worship life of the larger Church.

It is our hope that praying and singing the prayers and canticles in this collection will deepen and strengthen our encounter with Christ and make it possible, with ever increasing conviction, to cry out with St. Ambrose, "You have shown yourself to me, O Christ, face to face. I have met you in your sacraments."

# Introduction

In 1789, the fledgling Episcopal Church, meeting in Philadelphia, adopted the first American Book of Common Prayer. Explaining its departure in certain respects from the BCP of the Church of England, its preface observes that

> It is a most invaluable part of that blessed "liberty wherewith Christ hath made us free," that in his worship different forms and usages may without offense be allowed, provided the substance of the Faith be kept entire...therefore, by common consent and authority, may be altered, abridged, enlarged, amended, or otherwise disposed of, as may seem most convenient for the edification of the people, "according to the various exigency of times and occasions."

Since that historic decision, our Church has continued to seek an authorized language of Common Prayer capable of expressing what we believe about God, as well as reflecting on our own corporate and individual relationship to the Godhead. In formulating language for our prayers to the Trinity, we come to know God more closely. The decision to provide contemporary language rites in the 1979 Book of Common Prayer was a reaffirmation of the principles stated in that original American preface. The subsequent decade saw further efforts to produce supplemental rites in an American vernacular which would expand the language and metaphors we use to speak of and to God. This expansiveness has been more than an attempt to reflect current concerns with, say, gender issues or the transformation of society from a predominantly rural culture to an urban one; though assuredly it addresses these vital matters. Yet in trying to come closer to our experiences of God throughout the ages, it also often returns to the resonant imagery of earlier periods in the Church's history —in particular the writings of the Early Church, along with the ecstatic evocations of the Medieval mystics—sometimes neglected by liturgies in recent centuries.

In 1997, the General Convention of the Episcopal Church, again meeting in Philadelphia, authorized *Enriching Our Worship*, the fourth edition of *Supplemental Liturgical Materials*. This new book contains all the expansive language texts currently authorized, superseding all previous editions which should no longer be used. Inclusive/expansive language has developed considerably since those early efforts published in *Prayer Book Studies 30*. Then as now, ears attuned to contemporary language and culture grew uncomfortable with liturgical metaphors and forms of address, inherited largely from the 18th and 19th centuries, in which God is primarily envisioned as a kind of *Paterfamilias*. However, the search for remedies has not been smooth. Both positive and negative reactions to early experiments emphasized that a substantial number of Episcopalians are most wary of language which strikes them as abstract or depersonalizing (hence the widespread distaste for "Creator/Redeemer/Sanctifier" even among those who do not find the formulation modalist). A fairly conservative fellow-parishioner once said to me, "I would rather call God 'Mother' than something neutral." People frequently greet fresh images with enthusiasm when those expressions seem illuminating—the new may well be absorbed more readily than minor alterations in familiar texts. At the same time, however, worshipers need to be able to relate unfamiliar words and metaphors to some context, so that the language expresses the prayer of the people of God. With some people, a major sense of context will spring from life experiences; others look for continuity with biblical and ecclesiastical tradition. Keeping these various points in mind, the introduction to the notes in this volume explains how the new texts draw upon some of the riches of scripture and the Christian tradition, which include an abundance of images of

God. The committee sought language and imagery which would speak to the diversity of people who worship in the Episcopal Church today, both those who are well steeped in the tradition and those whose knowledge of scripture and the Christian tradition is fragmentary and to whom much traditional liturgical language is puzzling. The goal was to employ evocative language which would lead worshipers deeper into the mystery of God.

*Enriching Our Worship* adds significantly to the body of texts already available in the 1996 edition of *Supplemental Liturgical Materials*. Taking into consideration evaluations received from congregations who have used earlier editions, we have also revised certain texts, and removed those notes which seemed, in retrospect, to merely editorialize. Notes identifying sources, or containing substantive explanations helpful to the users, have been left intact. Where evaluations had indicated some confusion in celebrating the rite, annotations were appended for clarification. Following the practice of the 1991 and 1996 editions of *Supplemental Liturgical Materials*, *Enriching Our Worship* avoids supplying complete rites, providing instead a collection of texts, any one (or several) of which may be incorporated into a Rite Two Eucharist, Morning or Evening Prayer.

In determining those directions new texts should take, we also looked at some recent, widely used materials from other branches of the Church. In particular, we considered *A New Zealand Prayer Book* (1989), *Celebrating Common Prayer* (1992), and the 1994 Psalter and Canticles produced by the Roman Catholic International Consultation on English in the Liturgy (ICEL). Consulting these three volumes, we borrowed directly or, in certain cases, adapted, 16 new canticles. Thirteen are taken from scriptural sources. We have included such texts as "A Song of the Wilderness" (Isaiah 35: 1-7, 10); "A Song of Jerusalem Our Mother" (Isaiah 66: 10-14); "A Song of Our Adoption" (Ephesians 1:3-10); "A Song of God's Love" (I John 4:7-11); and "A Song of the Heavenly City" (Revelation 21:22-26, 22:1-4). In addition, we have included three non-scriptural canticles: Anselm of Canterbury's "A Song of Christ's Goodness"; and two passages from Julian of Norwich—"A Song of True Motherhood" and "A

Song of Our True Nature;" all three come from *Celebrating Common Prayer*. A table of "Suggested Canticles at Morning and Evening Prayer," employing some of these offerings enriches the list in the 1979 Book of Common Prayer. A new version of the *Venite* directly addresses God in the manner of already available variants for The Song of Zechariah and The Song of Mary (ELLC). Also included is a fresh translation of The Song of Hannah, and a metrical version of the "Phos hilaron" (from *Celebrating Common Prayer*). In both eucharistic and office rites, we have included, as an option for the conclusion of the lessons, "Hear what the Spirit is saying to God's people" or "Hear what the Spirit is saying to the Churches"; to which the congregation may respond, "Thanks be to God." These options are based on Christ's command to the seven Churches in Asia Minor from the Book of Revelation (2:29, 3:13, 22).

The final item adapted from other sources is a contemporary language version of "The Great Litany" (based on the text appearing in *An Alternative Prayer Book, 1984, According to the Use of the Church of Ireland* and *Celebrating Common Prayer*). The 1979 BCP continues to follow a longstanding tradition which substitutes, for those passages referring to the British Monarch, intercessions for "the President of the United States and all others in authority." Some have felt that this formulation does not really reflect the tripartite nature of our country's government. Therefore, the adapted version makes specific mention of legislative, executive and judicial branches, at national, state and local levels. The new version can be sung to the traditional chant. It is hoped that this contemporary version of the Litany may give many people a fresh understanding of its petitions.

Some new collects are derived from ancient sources like the Gelasian Sacramentary, the Veronese Sacramentary, and Alcuin of York's Mass of Wisdom. A short prayer by St. Gertrude the Great marks the beginning of a project to include devotions by some of the Mothers of the Church in the same way the BCP has preserved prayers of St. John Chrysostom, St. Francis of Assisi, and other Church Fathers. A few collects are newly composed, employing some scriptural imagery underrepresented by what has been currently available. All these may be used in place of the collect for the day, or, alternatively, *post precum*. One collect is borrowed from *A New Zealand Prayerbook* because it ties in with creation imagery expressed in Job 38:4-11, which we have used in a new eucharistic prayer.

The language of this prayer is biblical in a characteristic Anglican mode, yet also conveys a contemporary intimacy in the way God is addressed. As the notes explain, its structure is patterned on the one Thomas Talley discerns underlying

> the diversity of classical eucharistic prayers in both the eastern and western liturgical traditions prior to the Reformation.
>
> In this classical pattern of eucharistic prayer, praise to the Creator leads into the *Sanctus*. This is followed by thanksgiving for redemption, climaxing in the narrative of the institution and leading into a memorial oblation...Following this oblation, the prayer shifts to supplication, with an invocation of the Holy Spirit upon the bread and wine and upon the gathered community.
>
> To underscore that the institution narrative is part of the thanksgiving for redemption, this eucharistic prayer introduces the institution narrative with the words "We thank you." To strengthen the unity of the thanksgiving for redemption and the memorial oblation, an acclamation by the people follows the oblation and leads into the supplication.

In addition, a new confession of sin has been provided, along with two postcommunion prayers. Two concluding blessings have been taken from Celtic sources. A final one, from St. Clare, adds another prayer from a Mother of the Church.

The ultimate aim of expansive language experiments in the Episcopal Church is to create a language of prayer for all God's people. To this end, we consulted congregations who had used *Supplemental Liturgical Materials* in the past, but also reached out to solicit a spectrum of opinion among Anglicans of many traditions, including Anglo-Catholics, Evangelicals, and Charismatics ("Hear what the Spirit is saying to the Church" is a proclamation heard in certain Pentecostal traditions). The opinions of theologians, seminary and monastic communities, ecumenical liturgists and poets were also sought. Their comments have been constructive, and influenced the shape of these texts.

*Enriching Our Worship* marks only one more step in an ongoing process of development. Though much has been accomplished during the last decade, the development of expansive language liturgies is still at an early stage. More remains to be done. Perhaps the greatest stumbling block to progress is a real shortage of feedback. Many in our Church have yet to encounter *Supplemental Liturgical Materials*, if they have even heard of it. Some of those who use, or have at least tried it, don't bother to report their reactions. Nor do groups engaged in writing new liturgies often share them with the Standing Commission on Liturgy and Music (the successor body to the Standing Liturgical Commission and the Standing Commission on Church Music). Calls for such work often get little or no response. In order to faithfully continue the process of discernment needed to develop new prayers expressing the worship of God's people, the Standing Commission on Liturgy and Music needs to hear from all parts of the Church. And as we pray these new rites, we should remember the spirit of the injunction from the 1789 preface to the first American Book of Common Prayer, to receive and examine them in a candid, charitable spirit, without prejudices or presuppositions, "seriously considering what Christianity is, and what the truths of the Gospel are," asking the divine and eternal Word for words to best praise and petition our God who is the author of all creation.

*Phoebe Pettingell*
for the Standing Commission on Liturgy and Music

# The Use of Supplemental Liturgical Materials

*Enriching Our Worship* contains texts intended to be explorations for the development of liturgical materials reflective of the diversity of the Church and looking forward to the dissemination throughout the Church of a richer fabric of liturgical expression. Especially for congregations new to this material, a three-step process will provide an ordered entry into the exploration. The steps are preparation, use and evaluation.

## 1. *Preparation*

All liturgy is based upon a set of agreed-upon assumptions. Whenever those assumptions are altered, there is the possibility of congregational reaction ranging from confusion to anger. The introduction of new liturgical texts demands careful preparation and pastoral sensitivity. Use of these prayers in any community must be accompanied by time for exploring issues raised by their use and time for reflection before, during and after their use in worship. One way to begin the introduction of the new texts is to use them with small groups who can study the texts before they are used and begin to obtain some familiarity with them before they are used as a principal serviced on Sunday. Another strategy is to carefully announce the use of new texts at a regularly scheduled congregational liturgy, simultaneously announcing opportunities to reflect on the experience in an atmosphere of non-threatening dialogue.

Designing liturgies using supplemental liturgical materials will require careful and thorough planning. Decisions will have to be made as to what texts are to be used. There needs to be a conscious decision to use the texts long enough for worshipers to gain some familiarity with the prayers. Texts need to be used for a sufficient period of time to determine which prayers engage, nourish, and sustain a particular community in its relationship to God. Only after using the texts for a significant period of time can the community discern their applicability to its prayer life.

### 2. The Use of Supplemental Liturgical Materials

Supplemental liturgical materials may only be used with the permission of the diocesan bishop or, in the absence of the bishop, of the appropriate ecclesiastical authority. This authorization has a twofold purpose. First, it recognizes and affirms the bishop as the expression of unity in the life of the Church. Secondly, it provides a point of dialogue for the ongoing experience and development of the rites. Liturgical development needs to be done within the purview of the whole Church where there is a framework for theological reflection and dialogue.

These materials are intended to be resources for the life of the Church. The texts may be used in two very different ways. First, any of the texts may be used in conjunction with the Rite Two liturgies of the 1979 BCP. For instance, the canticles may be used in the context of a Rite Two Morning or Evening Prayer or as an alternative to the *Song of Praise* in the Eucharist. Or, one of the supplemental eucharistic prayers may be used with a Rite Two Eucharist. A second option is to develop an entire liturgy using the supplemental texts. The entire eucharistic liturgy can be designed with only the collect of the day from the BCP being added. Either of these options can be authorized for a principal Sunday morning service.

Decisions must be made on what materials need to be in the hands of the congregation. For a minimal application of the new texts, a simple insertion of the text in a bulletin will suffice. For the circumstance in which an entire liturgy is built from new materials a complete service booklet will need to be developed. Copyright is extended to congregations for the reproduction of the texts included in *Enriching Our Worship*.

Those who preside over the prayer of the community have a particular responsibility to study and reflect upon the prayers. One needs to read and to meditate upon these texts prior to voicing them as the prayer of the whole community.

An Order for Celebrating the Holy Eucharist, found on page 400 of the BCP, may also be used in conjunction with the "Forms for the Eucharistic Prayer" in the supplemental materials. This option provides a means whereby groups who wish to begin to write their own prayers may use them in worship, except at the principal service on Sunday. New texts might include collects, forms for the prayers of the people, postcommunion prayers, canticles, etc. The "Forms for the Eucharistic Prayer" provide a framework of the traditional elements of a eucharistic prayer which can be used as a basis for new expressions of thanksgiving and praise.

Congregations who may not have the gifts to compose extensive texts might explore a few options which are flexible under the rubrics of the BCP. The option to evolve prayers of the people within a congregation has been in place since the advent of the 1979 BCP. A list of general intercessory categories can be found on page 383 of the BCP, but the form and language of the intercession may be written in and for a local congregation. Gathering members of the congregation to write intercessory prayer and develop skills in the writing of texts is a creative way to engage the life of the whole community. When crafting forms for intercessory prayer, it is recommended that a common congregational response be used on a consistent basis, so that the text can easily change from Sunday to Sunday. Further suggestions on the prayers of the people are found in *Enriching Our Worship*. The collect at the conclusion of the prayers of the people is not a prescribed collect. Those congregations who are in the process of developing prayers may use this opportunity to explore new options.

Music is a major consideration in designing any liturgy. Hymn texts offer diverse ways to speak of God. There is a body of hymnody in *The Hymnal 1982* which expands our language for God and is consistent with the supplemental texts in regard to references to human beings. For instance, Hymn 371 praises the Holy Trinity in non-gender-related language. Often metrical settings of psalms and canticles reflect modern linguistic changes and are appropriate when designing liturgies using the supplemental texts. *Wonder, Love and Praise,* a supplement to *The Hymnal 1982,* recently published by Church Publishing, Inc., adds considerably to the diversity of musical material available for liturgical use. Music is also available for Eucharistic Prayers 1, 2 and 3 in this volume.

Even though women are included as ordained ministers and as lectors, intercessors, and acolytes, they still are all too often invisible in our worshiping communities. The choice of lectionary readings in the Episcopal Eucharistic Lectionary has often deleted or diminished the place of women in salvation history. *The Revised Common Lectionary* is authorized for trial use. This lectionary seeks to expand the scripture appointed for the Sunday Eucharist to include passages which reflect the faithful witness of women. Congregations using the supplemental materials might explore the use of this lectionary.

The context in which the supplemental liturgical materials are used will shape the experience of these prayers. Non-verbal language—the language of gesture, movement, sign—will always override the text of the prayer. Therefore, care needs to be taken on the setting of these prayers. Liturgical ministry should reflect the fullness of the worshiping community.

*3. Evaluation*

All liturgical texts are rich in what they say about God but also what they say about ourselves in relationship with God. This is at the heart of any theological reflection upon the experience of liturgical prayer. Who does the text say God is, who does it say we are, and—most importantly—what does this mean for us? These questions form the basis upon which the community can explore how these prayers speak in the hearts, minds, and spirit of the community of faith.

You are encouraged to communicate your experience of these materials to the Office for Liturgy and Music at the Episcopal Church Center, 815 Second Avenue, New York, NY 10017. The office is especially interested to receive materials written locally, for a particular congregation's worship. It is only as materials are collected and evaluated that the whole Church will begin to have prayers which expand the breadth and depth of the Church's prayer life.

### A View to the Future

The task for the Church is not merely to translate but to find the voice of prayer in the heart, spirit and mind of the people praying. The process of enriching our prayer is by nature an extended process requiring use, evaluation and theological reflection. As the process unfolds, new questions are raised and new avenues of expression are disclosed. General Convention Resolution C021s directs the Standing Commission on Liturgy and Music to *prepare a plan for liturgical revision and enrichment of the common worship of this Church.* The resolution also directs the commission to consider the Church's...*multicultural, multiethnic, multilingual and multigenerational*...constituency, in the process of...*providing rites and structures that ensure the unity of Common Prayer.*

This is not a task the commission can complete without the help of local worshiping communities. Whatever we imagine the future of the Book of Common Prayer to be, the task in the months and years to come is to compose, use, evaluate and distribute a wide variety of emerging resources. You are invited to share in that process.

# Morning and Evening Prayer

## Opening Sentences

*Advent*

Arise, O Jerusalem, stand upon the height and look toward the east, and see your children gathered from west and east at the word of the Holy One. *Baruch 5:5*

*Advent*

Shower, O heavens, from above, and let the skies rain down righteousness; let the earth open, that salvation may spring up, and let it cause righteousness to sprout up also. *Isaiah 45:8*, NRSV

*Christmas*

The Word became flesh and dwelt among us, full of grace and truth. *John 1:14*

*Lent*

Jesus said: "If any of you would come after me, deny yourself and take up your cross and follow me." *Mark 8:34*

*Holy Week*

Christ Jesus, being found in human form, humbled himself and became obedient unto death, even death on a cross.
*Philippians 2:8*

*Easter*

If anyone is in Christ, there is a new creation: everything old has passed away; see, everything has become new! *2 Corinthians 5:17*, NRSV

*Occasions of Thanksgiving*

We give you thanks, O God, we give you thanks, calling upon your Name and declaring all your wonderful deeds. *Psalm 75:1*

*All Saints and Major Saints' Days*

You are no longer strangers and sojourners, but citizens together with the saints and members of the household of God. *Ephesians 2:19*

*At Any Time*

God is Spirit, and those who worship must worship in spirit and in truth. *John 4:24*

# Confession

*The Deacon or Celebrant says*

Let us confess our sins to God.

*Silence may be kept.*

*Minister and People*

God of all mercy,
we confess that we have sinned against you,
opposing your will in our lives.
We have denied your goodness in each other,
in ourselves, and in the world you have created.
We repent of the evil that enslaves us,
    the evil we have done,
and the evil done on our behalf.
Forgive, restore, and strengthen us
through our Savior Jesus Christ,
that we may abide in your love
and serve only your will. Amen.

# Absolution

Almighty God have mercy on you, forgive you all your sins through the grace of Jesus Christ, strengthen you in all goodness, and by the power of the Holy Spirit keep you in eternal life. *Amen.*

# Opening Versicle

## Morning Prayer

*Officiant*　　O God, let our mouth proclaim your praise.
*People*　　And your glory all the day long.

## Evening Prayer

*Officiant*　　O God, be not far from us.
*People*　　Come quickly to help us, O God.

# Doxology

Praise to the holy and undivided Trinity, one God: as it was in the beginning, is now, and will be for ever. Amen.

*Except in Lent add*　Alleluia.

## Antiphons on Venite or Jubilate

*In Advent*

Our God and Savior now draws near: O come let us worship.

*From the Epiphany through the Baptism of Christ, and on the Feasts of the Transfiguration and Holy Cross*

Christ has shown forth his glory: O come let us worship.

*In Lent*

Our God is full of compassion and mercy: O come let us worship.

*or this*

Today, if you would hear God's voice: harden not your hearts.

*From Easter Day until the Ascension*

Alleluia. Christ is risen. O come let us worship. Alleluia.

*On Trinity Sunday*

The holy and undivided Trinity, one God: O come let us worship.

*On other Sundays*

Christ has triumphed over death: O come let us worship.

*On other Sundays and Weekdays*

God is the Rock of our salvation: O come let us worship.

*or this*

The Holy One is in our midst: O come let us worship.

*On All Saints and other Major Saints' Days*

*The bracketed Alleluias in this Antiphon are used only in Easter Season.*

[Alleluia.] Our God is glorious in all the saints: O come let us worship. [Alleluia.]


# Invitatory Psalms


## Venite *Psalm 95:1-7*

Come, let us sing to the Lord; *
 let us shout for joy to the Rock of our salvation.
Let us come before God's presence with thanksgiving *
 and raise to the Lord a shout with psalms.
For you are a great God; *
 you are great above all gods.
In your hand are the caverns of the earth, *
 and the heights of the hills are yours also.

The sea is yours, for you made it, *
   and your hands have molded the dry land.
Come, let us bow down and bend the knee, *
   and kneel before the Lord our Maker.
For you are our God,
and we are the people of your pasture and the sheep of your hand. *
   Oh, that today we would hearken to your voice!

*The following verses are added when Psalm 95 is used as the Invitatory:*

Let us listen today to God's voice:
Harden not your hearts,
as your forebears did in the wilderness, *
   at Meribah, and on that day at Massah,
   when they tempted me.
They put me to the test, *
   though they had seen my works.
Forty years long I detested that generation and said, *
   "This people are wayward in their hearts;
   they do not know my ways."
So I swore in my wrath, *
   "They shall not enter into my rest."

# Morning Psalms

*In place of an Invitatory Psalm, one of the following Morning Psalms may be sung or said.*

*Suggested Antiphons for use with these Psalms will be found on page 24.*

### Psalm 63:1-8 *Deus, Deus meus*

O God, you are my God; eagerly I seek you; *
   my soul thirsts for you, my flesh faints for you,
   as in a barren and dry land where there is no water.
Therefore I have gazed upon you in your holy place, *
   that I might behold your power and your glory.
For your loving-kindness is better than life itself; *
   my lips shall give you praise.

So will I bless you as long as I live *
   and lift up my hands in your Name.
My soul is content, as with marrow and fatness, *
   and my mouth praises you with joyful lips,
When I remember you upon my bed, *
   and meditate on you in the night watches.
For you have been my helper, *
   and under the shadow of your wings I will rejoice.
My soul clings to you; *
   your right hand holds me fast.

## Psalm 67:1-5 *Deus misereatur*

O God, be merciful to us and bless us, *
   show us the light of your countenance and come to us.
Let your ways be known upon earth, *
   your saving health among all nations.
Let the peoples praise you, O God; *
   let all the peoples praise you.
Let the nations be glad and sing for joy, *
   for you judge the peoples with equity
   and guide all the nations upon earth.
Let the peoples praise you, O God; *
   let all the peoples praise you.


# Evening Psalms

## Light of the World *Phos hilaron*

Light of the world, in grace and beauty,
Mirror of God's eternal face,
Transparent flame of love's free duty,
You bring salvation to our race.
Now, as we see the lights of evening,
We raise our voice in hymns of praise;
Worthy are you of endless blessing,
Sun of our night, lamp of our days.

*In place of or in addition to, Phos hilaron or some other hymn, one of the following Evening Psalms may be sung or said.*

*Suggested Antiphons for use with these Psalms will be found below.*

## Psalm 134 *Ecce nunc*

Behold now, bless the LORD, all you servants of the LORD, *
  you that stand by night in the house of the LORD.
Lift up your hands in the holy place and bless the LORD; *
  the LORD who made heaven and earth bless you out of Zion.

## Psalm 141:1-3,8ab *Domine, clamavi*

O LORD, I call to you; come to me quickly; *
  hear my voice when I cry to you.
Let my prayer be set forth in your sight as incense, *
  the lifting up of my hands as the evening sacrifice.
Set a watch before my mouth, O LORD,
and guard the door of my lips; *
  let not my heart incline to any evil thing.
My eyes are turned to you, Lord GOD; *
  in you I take refuge.

## Antiphons for Morning and Evening Psalms

*On Psalm 63*

O God, you are my God; from break of day I seek you.

*On Psalm 67*

Let the peoples praise you, O God; let all the peoples praise you.

*or*

Day by day we bless you; we praise your name for ever.

*On Psalm 134*

Yours is the day, O God, yours also the night; you established the moon and the sun.

*On Psalm 141*
Let my prayer be set forth in your sight as incense, the lifting up of my hands as the evening sacrifice.

*In the seasons of Advent, Christmas, Lent, and Easter, and on Holy Days, antiphons drawn from the opening sentences given in the Offices, or from other passages of Scripture, may be used instead.*

# The Lessons

*After the Readings, the Reader may say*

> Hear what the Spirit is saying to God's people.
> *or*
> Hear what the Spirit is saying to the Churches.

*People*     Thanks be to God.

# Canticle 12

## A Song of Creation *Benedicite, omnia opera Domini*
*Song of the Three, 35–65*

*One or more sections of this Canticle may be used. Whatever the selection, it begins with the Invocation and concludes with the Doxology.*

*Invocation*

Glorify the Lord, all you works of the Lord, *
    sing praise and give honor for ever.
In the high vault of heaven, glorify the Lord, *
    sing praise and give honor for ever.

*I. The Cosmic Order*

Glorify the Lord, you angels and all powers of the Lord, *
    O heavens and all waters above the heavens.
Sun and moon and stars of the sky, glorify the Lord, *
    sing praise and give honor for ever.

Glorify the Lord, every shower of rain and fall of dew, *
    all winds and fire and heat.

Winter and summer, glorify the Lord, *
  sing praise and give honor for ever.

Glorify the Lord, O chill and cold, *
  drops of dew and flakes of snow.
Frost and cold, ice and sleet, glorify the Lord, *
  sing praise and give honor for ever.

Glorify the Lord, O nights and days, *
  O shining light and enfolding dark.
Storm clouds and thunderbolts, glorify the Lord, *
  sing praise and give honor for ever.

II. *The Earth and Its Creatures*

Let the earth glorify the Lord, *
  sing praise and give honor for ever.
Glorify the Lord, O mountains
and hills, and all that grows upon the earth, *
  sing praise and give honor for ever.

Glorify the Lord, O springs of water, seas, and streams, *
  O whales and all that move in the waters.
All birds of the air, glorify the Lord, *
  sing praise and give honor for ever.

Glorify the Lord, O beasts of the wild, *
  and all you flocks and herds.
O men and women everywhere, glorify the Lord, *
  sing praise and give honor for ever.

III. *The People of God*

Let the people of God glorify the Lord, *
  sing praise and give honor for ever.
Glorify the Lord, O priests and servants of the Lord, *
  sing praise and give honor for ever.

Glorify the Lord, O spirits and souls of the righteous, *
  sing praise and give honor for ever.
You that are holy and humble of heart, glorify the Lord, *
  sing praise and give honor for ever.

*Doxology*

Let us glorify the Lord: Father, Son and Holy Spirit; *
    sing praise and give honor for ever.
In the high vault of heaven, glorify the Lord, *
    sing praise and give honor for ever.

# Canticle 15

## The Song of Mary *Magnificat*

My soul proclaims the greatness of the Lord,
my spirit rejoices in you, O God my Savior, *
    for you have looked with favor on your lowly servant.
From this day all generations will call me blessed: *
    you, the Almighty, have done great things for me,
    and holy is your name.
You have mercy on those who fear you *
    from generation to generation.
You have shown strength with your arm *
    and scattered the proud in their conceit,
Casting down the mighty from their thrones *
    and lifting up the lowly.
You have filled the hungry with good things *
    and sent the rich away empty.
You have come to the help of your servant Israel, *
    for you have remembered your promise of mercy,
The promise made to our forebears, *
    to Abraham and his children for ever.

# Canticle 16

## The Song of Zechariah *Benedictus Dominus Deus*

Blessed are you, Lord, the God of Israel, *
    you have come to your people and set them free.
You have raised up for us a mighty Savior, *
    born of the house of your servant David.

Through your holy prophets you promised of old
to save us from our enemies, *
   from the hands of all who hate us,
To show mercy to our forebears, *
   and to remember your holy covenant.
This was the oath you swore to our father Abraham, *
   to set us free from the hands of our enemies,
Free to worship you without fear, *
   holy and righteous before you,
   all the days of our life.
And you, child, shall be called the prophet
    of the Most High, *
   for you will go before the Lord to prepare the way,
To give God's people knowledge of salvation *
   by the forgiveness of their sins.
In the tender compassion of our God *
   the dawn from on high shall break upon us,
To shine on those who dwell in darkness
    and the shadow of death, *
   and to guide our feet into the way of peace.

# Canticle 18

**A Song to the Lamb** *Dignus es*
*Revelation 4:11;5:9-10,13*

Splendor and honor and royal power *
   are yours by right, O God Most High,
For you created everything that is, *
   and by your will they were created and have their being;

And yours by right, O Lamb that was slain, *
   for with your blood you have redeemed for God,
From every family, language, people, and nation, *
   a royal priesthood to serve our God.

And so, to the One who sits upon the throne, *
    and to Christ the Lamb,
Be worship and praise, dominion and splendor, *
    for ever and for evermore.

# Canticle 21

**We Praise You, O God** *Te Deum laudamus*

We praise you, O God,
we acclaim you as Lord;
all creation worships you,
the Father everlasting.
To you all angels, all the powers of heaven,
the cherubim and seraphim, sing in endless praise:
    Holy, holy, holy Lord, God of power and might,
    heaven and earth are full of your glory.
The glorious company of apostles praise you.
The noble fellowship of prophets praise you.
The white-robed army of martyrs praise you.
Throughout the world the holy Church acclaims you:
    Father, of majesty unbounded,
    your true and only Son, worthy of all worship,
    and the Holy Spirit, advocate and guide.
You, Christ, are the king of glory,
the eternal Son of the Father.
When you took our flesh to set us free
you humbly chose the Virgin's womb.
You overcame the sting of death
and opened the kingdom of heaven to all believers.
You are seated at God's right hand in glory.
We believe that you will come to be our judge.
    Come then, Lord, and help your people,
    bought with the price of your own blood,
    and bring us with your saints
    to glory everlasting.

# Canticle A

## A Song of Wisdom *Sapientia liberavit*
*Wisdom 10:15-19,20b-21*

Wisdom freed from a nation of oppressors *
  a holy people and a blameless race.
She entered the soul of a servant of the Lord, *
  withstood dread rulers with wonders and signs.

To the saints she gave the reward of their labors, *
  and led them by a marvelous way;
She was their shelter by day *
  and a blaze of stars by night.

She brought them across the Red Sea, *
  she led them through mighty waters;
But their enemies she swallowed in the waves *
  and spewed them out from the depths of the abyss.

And then, Lord, the righteous sang hymns to your Name, *
  and praised with one voice your protecting hand;
For Wisdom opened the mouths of the mute, *
  and gave speech to the tongues of a new-born people.

# Canticle B

## A Song of Pilgrimage *Priusquam errarem*
*Ecclesiasticus 51:13-16,20b-22*

Before I ventured forth,
even while I was very young, *
  I sought wisdom openly in my prayer.
In the forecourts of the temple I asked for her, *
  and I will seek her to the end.
From first blossom to early fruit, *
  she has been the delight of my heart.
My foot has kept firmly to the true path, *
  diligently from my youth have I pursued her.
I inclined my ear a little and received her; *
  I found for myself much wisdom and became adept in her.

To the one who gives me wisdom will I give glory, *
  for I have resolved to live according to her way.
From the beginning I gained courage from her, *
  therefore I will not be forsaken.
In my inmost being I have been stirred to seek her, *
  therefore have I gained a good possession.
As my reward the Almighty has given me the gift of language,*
  and with it will I offer praise to God.


# Canticle C

## The Song of Hannah
*1 Samuel 2:1-8*

My heart exults in you, O God; *
  my triumph song is lifted in you.
My mouth derides my enemies, *
  for I rejoice in your salvation.
There is none holy like you, *
  nor any rock to be compared to you, our God.
Do not heap up prideful words or speak in arrogance; *
  Only God is knowing and weighs all actions.
The bows of the mighty are broken, *
  but the weak are clothed in strength.
Those once full now labor for bread, *
  those who hungered now are well fed.
The childless woman has borne sevenfold, *
  while the mother of many is forlorn.
God destroys and brings to life, casts down and raises up; *
  gives wealth or takes it away, humbles and dignifies.
God raises the poor from the dust; *
  and lifts the needy from the ash heap
To make them sit with the rulers *
  and inherit a place of honor.
For the pillars of the earth are God's *
  on which the whole earth is founded.

# Canticle D

## A Song of the Wilderness
*Isaiah 35:1-7,10*

The wilderness and the dry land shall be glad, *
  the desert shall rejoice and blossom;
It shall blossom abundantly, *
  and rejoice with joy and singing.
They shall see the glory of the Lord, *
  the majesty of our God.
Strengthen the weary hands, *
  and make firm the feeble knees.
Say to the anxious, "Be strong, do not fear! *
  Here is your God, coming with judgment to save you."
Then shall the eyes of the blind be opened, *
  and the ears of the deaf be unstopped.
Then shall the lame leap like a deer, *
  and the tongue of the speechless sing for joy.
For waters shall break forth in the wilderness *
  and streams in the desert;
The burning sand shall become a pool *
  and the thirsty ground, springs of water.
The ransomed of God shall return with singing, *
  with everlasting joy upon their heads.
Joy and gladness shall be theirs, *
  and sorrow and sighing shall flee away.

# Canticle E

## A Song of Jerusalem Our Mother
*Isaiah 66:10-14*

Rejoice with Jerusalem and be glad for her *
  all you who love her,
Rejoice, rejoice with her, *
  all you who mourn over her,

That you may drink deeply with delight *
    from her comforting breast.
For thus says our God, *
    "I will extend peace to her like a river,
    the wealth of nations like an overflowing stream.
"You shall nurse and be carried on her arm,
    and you shall nestle in her lap.
"As a mother comforts her child, so will I comfort you; *
    you shall be comforted in Jerusalem.
"You shall see, and your heart shall rejoice, *
    you shall flourish like the grass of the fields."

# Canticle F

## A Song of Lamentation
*Lamentations 1:12,16; 3:19,22-24,26*

Is it nothing to you, all you who pass by? *
    Look and see if there is any sorrow like my sorrow,
Which was brought upon me, *
    inflicted by God's fierce anger.
For these things I weep; my eyes flow with tears, *
    for a comforter is far from me, one to revive my courage.
Remember my affliction and my bitterness, *
    wormwood and gall!
The steadfast love of God never ceases, *
    God's mercies never end.
They are new every morning; *
    great is your faithfulness.
"God is my portion," says my soul, *
    "therefore will I hope in God."
It is good that we should wait quietly *
    for the coming of God's salvation.

# Canticle G

## A Song of Ezekiel
*Ezekiel 36:24-28*

I will take you from among all nations; *
    and gather you from all lands to bring you home.
I will sprinkle clean water upon you; *
    and purify you from false gods and uncleanness.
A new heart I will give you *
    and a new spirit put within you.
I will take the stone heart from your chest *
    and give you a heart of flesh.
I will help you walk in my laws *
    and cherish my commandments and do them.
You shall be my people, *
    and I will be your God.

# Canticle H

## A Song of Hosea
*Hosea 6:1-3*

Come, let us return to our God, *
    who has torn us and will heal us.
God has struck us and will bind up our wounds, *
    after two days revive us,
On the third day restore us, *
    that in God's presence we may live.
Let us humble ourselves, let us strive to know the Lord, *
    whose justice dawns like morning light,
    its dawning as sure as the sunrise.
God's justice will come to us like a shower, *
    like spring rains that water the earth.

# Canticle I

## A Song of Jonah
*Jonah 2:2-7,9*

I called to you, O God, out of my distress, and you answered me; *
    out of the belly of Sheol I cried, and you heard my voice.
You cast me into the deep, into the heart of the seas, *
    and the flood surrounded me;
    all your waves and billows passed over me.
Then I said, "I am driven away from your sight; *
    how shall I ever look again upon your holy temple?"
The waters closed in over me, the deep was round about me; *
    weeds were wrapped around my head at the roots of the mountains.
I went down to the land beneath the earth, *
    yet you brought up my life from the depths, O God.
As my life was ebbing away, I remembered you, O God, *
    and my prayer came to you, into your holy temple.
With the voice of thanksgiving, I will sacrifice to you; *
    what I have vowed I will pay, for deliverance belongs to the Lord!


# Canticle J

## A Song of Judith
*Judith 16:13-16*

I will sing a new song to my God, *
    for you are great and glorious, wonderful in strength, invincible.
Let the whole creation serve you, *
    for you spoke and all things came into being.
You sent your breath and it formed them, *
    no one is able to resist your voice.
Mountains and seas are stirred to their depths, *
    rocks melt like wax at your presence.
But to those who fear you, *
    you continue to show mercy.

No sacrifice, however fragrant, can please you, *
    but whoever fears the Lord shall stand in your sight for ever.

# Canticle K

## A Song of Our Adoption
*Ephesians 1:3-10*

Blessed are you, the God and Father of our Lord Jesus Christ, *
    for you have blessed us in Christ
    with every spiritual blessing in the heavenly places.
Before the world was made, you chose us to be yours in Christ, *
    that we should be holy and blameless before you.
You destined us for adoption as your children through Jesus Christ, *
    according to the good pleasure of your will,
To the praise of your glorious grace, *
    that you have freely given us in the Beloved.
In you, we have redemption through the blood of Christ,
    the forgiveness of our sins,
According to the riches of your grace *
    which you have lavished upon us.
You have made known to us, in all wisdom and insight, *
    the mystery of your will,
According to your good pleasure which you set forth in Christ, *
    as a plan for the fullness of time,
To gather together all things in Christ, *
    things in heaven and things on earth.

# Canticle L

## A Song of Christ's Humility
*Philippians 2:6-11*

Though in the form of God, *
    Christ Jesus did not cling to equality with God,
But emptied himself, taking the form of a servant, *
    and was born in human likeness.
Being found in human form, he humbled himself *
    and became obedient to death, even death on a cross.

Therefore, God has highly exalted him *
  and given him the name above every name,
That at the name of Jesus, every knee shall bow, *
  in heaven and on earth and under the earth,
And every tongue confess that Jesus Christ is Lord, *
  to the glory of God the Father.

# Canticle M

## A Song of Faith
*1 Peter 1:3-4,18-21*

Blessed be the God and Father of our Lord Jesus Christ, *
  by divine mercy we have a new birth into a living hope;
Through the resurrection of Jesus Christ from the dead, *
  we have an inheritance that is imperishable in heaven.
The ransom that was paid to free us *
  was not paid in silver or gold,
But in the precious blood of Christ, *
  the Lamb without spot or stain.
God raised Jesus from the dead and gave him glory *
  so that we might have faith and hope in God.

# Canticle N

## A Song of God's Love
*1 John 4:7-11*

Beloved, let us love one another, *
  for love is of God.
Whoever does not love does not know God, *
  for God is Love.
In this the love of God was revealed among us, *
  that God sent his only Son into the world,
  so that we might live through Jesus Christ.

In this is love, not that we loved God but that God loved us *
　　and sent his Son that sins might be forgiven.
Beloved, since God loved us so much, *
　　we ought also to love one another.
For if we love one another, God abides in us, *
　　and God's love will be perfected in us.


# Canticle O

### A Song of the Heavenly City
*Revelation 21:22-26, 22:1-4*

I saw no temple in the city, *
　　for its temple is the God of surpassing strength and the Lamb.
And the city has no need of sun or moon to light it, *
　　for the glory of God shines on it, and its lamp is the Lamb.
By its light the nations shall walk, *
　　and the rulers of the world lay their honor and glory there.
Its gates shall never be shut by day, nor shall there be any night; *
　　into it they will bring the honor and glory of nations.
I saw the clean river of the water of life, bright as crystal, *
　　flowing from the throne of God and of the Lamb.
The tree of life spanned the river, giving fruit every month, *
　　and the leaves of the tree were for the healing of nations.
All curses cease where the throne of God and the Lamb stands,
and all servants give worship there; *
　　there they will see God's face, whose Name shall be on their foreheads.


# Canticle P

### A Song of the Spirit
*Revelation 22:12-17*

"Behold, I am coming soon," says the Lord,
"and bringing my reward with me, *
　　to give to everyone according to their deeds.

"I am the Alpha and the Omega, the first and the last, *
    the beginning and the end."
Blessed are those who do God's commandments,
that they may have the right to the tree of life, *
    and may enter the city through the gates.
"I, Jesus, have sent my angel to you, *
    with this testimony for all the churches.
"I am the root and the offspring of David, *
    I am the bright morning star."
"Come!" say the Spirit and the Bride; *
    "Come!" let each hearer reply!
Come forward, you who are thirsty, *
    let those who desire take the water of life as a gift.

# Canticle Q

## A Song of Christ's Goodness
*Anselm of Canterbury*

Jesus, as a mother you gather your people to you; *
    you are gentle with us as a mother with her children.
Often you weep over our sins and our pride, *
    tenderly you draw us from hatred and judgment.
You comfort us in sorrow and bind up our wounds, *
    in sickness you nurse us and with pure milk you feed us.
Jesus, by your dying, we are born to new life; *
    by your anguish and labor we come forth in joy.
Despair turns to hope through your sweet goodness; *
    through your gentleness, we find comfort in fear.
Your warmth gives life to the dead, *
    your touch makes sinners righteous.
Lord Jesus, in your mercy, heal us; *
    in your love and tenderness, remake us.
In your compassion, bring grace and forgiveness, *
    for the beauty of heaven, may your love prepare us.

# Canticle R

## A Song of True Motherhood
*Julian of Norwich*

God chose to be our mother in all things *
   and so made the foundation of his work,
     most humbly and most pure, in the Virgin's womb.
God, the perfect wisdom of all, *
   arrayed himself in this humble place.
Christ came in our poor flesh *
   to share a mother's care.
Our mothers bear us for pain and for death; *
   our true mother, Jesus, bears us for joy and endless life.
Christ carried us within him in love and travail, *
   until the full time of his passion.
And when all was completed and he had carried us so for joy, *
   still all this could not satisfy the power of his wonderful love.
All that we owe is redeemed in truly loving God, *
   for the love of Christ works in us;
     Christ is the one whom we love.

# Canticle S

## A Song of Our True Nature
*Julian of Norwich*

Christ revealed our frailty and our falling, *
   our trespasses and our humiliations.
Christ also revealed his blessed power, *
   his blessed wisdom and love.
He protects us as tenderly and as sweetly when we are in greatest need; *
   he raises us in spirit
     and turns everything to glory and joy without ending.

God is the ground and the substance, the very essence of nature; *
   God is the true father and mother of natures.
We are all bound to God by nature, *
   and we are all bound to God by grace.
And this grace is for all the world, *
   because it is our precious mother, Christ.
For this fair nature was prepared by Christ
   for the honor and nobility of all, *
   and for the joy and bliss of salvation.


# The Apostles' Creed

I believe in God, the Father almighty,
   creator of heaven and earth.
I believe in Jesus Christ, God's only Son, our Lord,
   who was conceived by the Holy Spirit,
   born of the Virgin Mary,
   suffered under Pontius Pilate,
   was crucified, died, and was buried;
   he descended to the dead.
   On the third day he rose again;
   he ascended into heaven,
   he is seated at the right hand of the Father,
   and he will come again to judge the living and the dead.
I believe in the Holy Spirit,
   the holy catholic Church,
   the communion of saints,
   the forgiveness of sins,
   the resurrection of the body,
   and the life everlasting. Amen.

# Alternative to the Salutation

*The officiant introduces the prayer with one of the following.*

*Officiant* Hear our cry, O God.    *Officiant* God be with you.
*People*    And listen to our prayer.    *People*    And also with you.
*Officiant* Let us pray.    *Officiant* Let us pray.

# Suffrages For Use in Morning Prayer

V.   Help us, O God our Savior;
R.   Deliver us and forgive us our sins.
V.   Look upon your congregation;
R.   Give to your people the blessing of peace.
V.   Declare your glory among the nations;
R.   And your wonders among all peoples.
V.   Do not let the oppressed be shamed and turned away;
R.   Never forget the lives of your poor.
V.   Continue your loving-kindness to those who know you;
R.   And your favor to those who are true of heart.
V.   Satisfy us by your loving-kindness in the morning;
R.   So shall we rejoice and be glad all the days of our life.

# Concluding Sentence

Glory to God whose power, working in us, can do infinitely more
than we can ask or imagine: Glory to God from generation to
generation in the Church, and in Christ Jesus for ever and ever.
*Amen. Ephesians 3:20,21*

# Order of Worship for the Evening

## Opening Acclamations

*The Officiant greets the people with these words*

            Stay with us, Christ, for it is evening.
*People*    Make your Church bright with your radiance.

*In place of the above, from Easter Day through the Day of Pentecost*

*Officiant*    Christ is risen. Alleluia.
*People*    And has appeared to the disciples. Alleluia.

*In Lent and on other penitential occasions*

*Officiant*    Blessed be the God of our salvation:
*People*    Who bears our burdens and forgives our sins.

## Evening Psalms

*See page 23.*

## Blessings

*See page 70.*

# Suggested Canticles at Morning Prayer

## Supplemental Liturgical Materials and Rite II

|  | *After the Old Testament reading* | *After the New Testament reading* |
|---|---|---|
| **Sunday** | E. A song of Jerusalem Our Mother *or* 16. The Song of Zechariah | K. A Song of Our Adoption *or* 21. We Praise You O God |
|  | *Advent:* | *Advent:* |
|  | D. A song of the Wilderness | P. A Song of the Spirit |
|  | *Christmas:** | *Christmas:** |
|  | C. A Song of Hannah *or* 9. The First Song of Isaiah | N. A Song of God's Love *or* 20. Glory to God |
|  | *Lent:* | *Lent:* |
|  | H. A Song of Hosea | L. A Song of Christ's Humility |
|  | *Easter:* | *Easter:* |
|  | A. A Song of Wisdom *or* 8. The Song of Moses | M. A Song of Faith |
| **Monday** | C. A Song of Hannah *or* 11. The Third Song of Isaiah | L. A Song of Christ's Humility *or* Q. A Song of Christ's Goodness |
| **Tuesday** | B. A Song of Pilgrimage *or* 13. A Song of Praise | M. A Song of Faith *or* N. A Song of God's Love |
| **Wednesday** | G. A Song of Ezekiel *or* H. A Song of Hosea | P. A Song of the Spirit *or* S. A Song of Our True Nature |
|  | *Lent:* |  |
|  | I. A Song of Jonah *or* 10. The Second Song of Isaiah |  |
| **Thursday** | A. A Song of Wisdom *or* J. A Song of Judith | R. A Song of True Motherhood *or* 16. A Song of Zechariah |
| **Friday** | I. A Song of Jonah | 18. A Song to the Lamb |
|  | *Christmas:** | *Christmas:** |
|  | J. A Song of Judith | R. A Song of True Motherhood |
|  | *Lent:* | *Lent:* |
|  | F. A Song of Lamentation *or* 14. A Song of Penitence | S. A Song of Our True Nature |
|  | *Easter:* | *Easter:* |
|  | G. A Song of Ezekiel | K. A Song of Our Adoption |

| Saturday | 12. A Song of Creation *or* | O. A Song of the Heavenly City *or* |
|---|---|---|
| | D. A Song of the Wilderness | 19. The Song of the Redeemed |

*on Feasts of Our Lord and other Major Feasts*

| | 16. A Song of Zechariah *or* | 21. We Praise You O God *or* |
|---|---|---|
| | E. A Song of Jerusalem Our Mother | K. A Son of Our Adoption |

*Canticles appointed for Christmas may be used through the First Sunday after the Epiphany.*

# Suggested Canticles at Evening Prayer

## Supplemental Liturgical Materials and Rite II

| | After the Old Testament reading | After the New Testament reading |
|---|---|---|
| Sunday | 15. The Song of Mary | The Song of Simeon** *or* M. A Song of Faith** |
| Monday | A. A Song of Wisdom | N. A Song of God's Love *or* The Song of Simeon |
| Tuesday | D. A Song of the Wilderness | 15. The Song of Mary *or* P. A Song of the Spirit |
| Wednesday | C. The Song of Hannah | L. A Song of Christ's Humility *or* The Song of Simeon |
| Thursday | J. A Song of Judith | 15. The Song of Mary *or* S. A Song of Our True Nature |
| Friday | G. A Song of Ezekiel | Q. A Song of Christ's Goodness *or* The Song of Simeon |
| Saturday | B. A Song of Pilgrimage | 15. The Song of Mary *or* R. A Song of True Motherhood |

on Feasts of our Lord and other Major Feasts

| | 15. The Song of Mary | O. A Song of the Heavenly City** *or* The Song of Simeon** |
|---|---|---|

**If only one reading is used, the suggested canticle is The Song of Mary.*

# The Great Litany

*It is traditional to use sections I and VI. Other petitions may be added from sections II, III, IV and V. The first petition in section III is used as an introductory petition when petitions are included from section III, IV and/or V.*

I.

Holy God, Creator of heaven and earth,
*Have mercy on us.*

Holy and Mighty, Redeemer of the world,
*Have mercy on us.*

Holy Immortal One, Sanctifier of the faithful,
*Have mercy on us.*

Holy, blessed and glorious Trinity, One God,
*Have mercy on us.*

II.

From all evil and mischief; from pride, vanity and hypocrisy; from envy, hatred and malice; and from all evil intent,
*Savior deliver us.*

From sloth, worldliness and love of money; from hardness of heart and contempt for your word and your laws,
*Savior deliver us.*

From sins of body and mind; from deceits of the world, flesh and the devil,
*Savior deliver us.*

From famine and disaster; from violence, murder, and dying unprepared,
*Savior deliver us.*

In all times of sorrow; in all times of joy; in the hour of our death and at the day of judgment,
*Savior deliver us.*

By the mystery of your holy incarnation; by your birth, childhood and obedience; by your baptism, fasting and temptation,
*Savior deliver us.*

By your ministry in word and work; by your mighty acts of power; by the preaching of your reign,
*Savior deliver us.*

By your agony and trial; by your cross and passion; by your precious death and burial,
*Savior deliver us.*

By your mighty resurrection; by your glorious ascension; and by your sending of the Holy Spirit,
*Savior deliver us.*


III.
Hear our prayers, O Christ our God.
*Hear us, O Christ.*

Govern and direct your holy Church; fill it with love and truth; and grant it that unity which is your will.
*Hear us, O Christ.*

Give us boldness to preach the gospel in all the world, and to make disciples of all the nations.
*Hear us, O Christ.*

Enlighten your bishops, priests and deacons (especially _____) with knowledge and understanding, that by their teaching and their lives they may proclaim your word.
*Hear us, O Christ.*

Give your people grace to witness to your word and bring forth
the fruit of your Spirit.
*Hear us, O Christ.*

Bring into the way of truth all who have erred and are deceived.
*Hear us, O Christ.*

Strengthen those who stand; comfort and help the fainthearted;
raise up the fallen; and finally beat down Satan under our feet.
*Hear us, O Christ.*


IV.

Guide the leaders of the nations into the ways of peace and justice.
*Hear us, O Christ.*

Give your wisdom and strength to _____, the President of the
United States, _____ the Governor of this state, (and _____, the
Mayor of this city) that in all things they may do your will, for
your glory and the common good.
*Hear us, O Christ.*

Give to the Congress of the United States, the members of the
President's Cabinet, those who serve in our state legislature, and
all others in authority the grace to walk always in the ways of
truth.
*Hear us, O Christ.*

Bless the justices of the Supreme Court and all those who administer
the law, that they may act with integrity and do justice for all your
people.
*Hear us, O Christ.*

Give us the will to use the resources of the earth to your glory and
for the good of all.
*Hear us, O Christ.*

Bless and keep all your people,
*Hear us, O Christ.*

V.

Comfort and liberate the lonely, the bereaved (especially _____)
and the oppressed.
*Hear us, O Christ.*

Keep in safety those who travel (especially _____) and all who
are in peril.
*Hear us, O Christ.*

Heal the sick in body, mind or spirit (especially _____) and
provide for the homeless, the hungry and the destitute.
*Hear us, O Christ.*

Guard and protect all children who are in danger.
*Hear us, O Christ.*

Shower your compassion on prisoners, hostages and refugees, and
all who are in trouble.
*Hear us, O Christ.*

Forgive our enemies, persecutors and slanderers, and turn their
hearts.
*Hear us, O Christ.*

Hear us as we remember those who have died (especially _____)
and grant us with them a share in your eternal glory.
*Hear us, O Christ.*


VI.

Give us true repentance; forgive us our sins of negligence and
ignorance and our deliberate sins; and grant us the grace of your
Holy Spirit to amend our lives according to your word.
*Holy God,*
*Holy and Mighty,*
*Holy Immortal One,*
*Have mercy on us.*

# The Holy Eucharist

## Opening Acclamations

*Celebrant*  Blessed be the one, holy, and living God.
*People*  Glory to God for ever and ever.

*or*

*Celebrant*  Blessed be our God.
*People*  For ever and ever. Amen.

*During Advent*

*Celebrant*  Blessed are you, holy and living One.
*People*  You come to your people and set them free.

*From Easter Day through the Day of Pentecost*

*Celebrant*  Alleluia. Christ is risen.
*People*  Christ is risen indeed. Alleluia.

*In Lent and on other penitential occasions*

*Celebrant*  Blessed be the God of our salvation:
*People*  Who bears our burdens and forgives our sins.

# Song of Praise

*The rubrics of the Prayer Book (p. 356) provide that "some other song of praise" may be used in place of the hymn Gloria in excelsis. The supplemental canticles (pp. 25-41) or those in the Prayer Book (pp. 85-96) are among the appropriate alternatives.*

# Salutation

| | |
|---|---|
| *Celebrant* | God be with you. |
| *People* | And also with you. |
| *Celebrant* | Let us pray. |

# Collect of the Day

*During the season after the Epiphany and the season after Pentecost (except the First Sunday after the Epiphany, the Last Sunday after the Epiphany, Trinity Sunday and the Last Sunday after Pentecost, i.e., Proper 29), one of the following collects may be used instead of the appointed Collect of the Day:*

Christ our true and only Light: receive our morning prayers, and illumine the secrets of our hearts with your healing goodness, that no evil desires may possess us who are made new in the light of your heavenly grace. *Amen.*
(source: *Gelasian Sacramentary*)

O God our shield and armor of light, whom we adore with all the angelic host: defend us from evil; watch over any who are in danger this night and give your angels charge over them; and grant that we may always rejoice in your heavenly protection and serve you bravely in the world; through Jesus Christ our Savior. *Amen.*

Holy Wisdom, in your loving kindness you created and restored us when we were lost: inspire us with your truth, that we may love you with our whole minds and run to you with open hearts, through Christ our Savior. *Amen.*
(source: Alcuin of York, Mass of Wisdom)

God our rock and refuge: keep us safe in your care and strengthen us with your grace, that we may pray to you faithfully and love one another boldly, following the example of Jesus, who with you and the Holy Spirit lives for ever and ever. *Amen.*
(source: *Veronese Sacramentary*)

Sun of Righteousness, so gloriously risen, shine in our hearts as we celebrate our redemption, that we may see your way to our eternal home, where you reign, one holy and undivided Trinity, now and for ever. *Amen.*

Beloved God, as we approach your Presence, guide and stir us with your Holy Spirit, that we may become one body, one spirit in Jesus Christ our Savior. *Amen.*

Loving Jesus: Protect and sustain us with your hand. Open the door of your love that, sealed with your wisdom, we may be free to serve you with joy. *Amen.*
(a prayer of St. Gertrude)

Jesus, you are the way through the wilderness: show us your truth in which we journey, and by the grace of the Holy Spirit be in us the life that draws us to God. *Amen.*
(source: F.B. McNutt, *The Prayer Manual* [London: Mowbray, 1961], p. 29, adapted)

Jesus, the true bread that comes down from heaven: leaven us with your Holy Spirit, that the world may know the abundance of life in your new creation. *Amen.*

God of unchangeable power, when you fashioned the world the morning stars sang together and the host of heaven shouted for joy; open our eyes to the wonders of creation and teach us to use all things for good, to the honor of your glorious name; through Jesus Christ our Lord. *Amen.*
(source: *A New Zealand Prayer Book*, p. 569)

# Lessons

*After the Readings, the Reader may say*

         Hear what the Spirit is saying to God's people.
           *or*
         Hear what the Spirit is saying to the Churches.

*People*      Thanks be to God.

# Gospel Announcement

The Holy Gospel of our Savior Jesus Christ according to _____.

# Nicene Creed

We believe in one God,
  the Father, the Almighty,
  maker of heaven and earth,
  of all that is, seen and unseen.
We believe in one Lord, Jesus Christ,
  the only Son of God,
  eternally begotten of the Father,
  God from God, Light from Light,
  true God from true God,
  begotten, not made,
  of one Being with the Father;
  through him all things were made.
For us and for our salvation
    he came down from heaven,
    was incarnate of the Holy Spirit and the Virgin Mary
    and became truly human.
    For our sake he was crucified under Pontius Pilate;

he suffered death and was buried.
On the third day he rose again
in accordance with the Scriptures;
he ascended into heaven
and is seated at the right hand of the Father.
He will come again in glory to judge the living and the dead,
and his kingdom will have no end.
We believe in the Holy Spirit, the Lord, the giver of life,
who proceeds from the Father,
who with the Father and the Son is worshiped and glorified,
who has spoken through the prophets.
We believe in one holy catholic and apostolic Church.
We acknowledge one baptism for the forgiveness of sins.
We look for the resurrection of the dead,
and the life of the world to come. Amen.

# Prayers of the People

This book contains no forms for the Prayers of the People. Rather, it calls attention to the generous and flexible—and frequently overlooked—provisions of the Book of Common Prayer.

Of the six forms provided (BCP pp. 383–393), none are required. Any of them *may* be used or adapted to the occasion. They may also be replaced by other forms. All that is required is that the topics listed at the top of page 383 be included in the prayers.

The six forms provided may also be used as models for the creation of new forms. A few suggestions follow.

Form II has its roots in the practice of the Church in the earliest centuries. It consists simply of a series of biddings, covering the required topics (to which others may be added), each followed by silence. The intent is that the silences be long enough that the congregation is given opportunity for serious silent intercession.

Forms I and V follow the pattern of classical litanies, and are in each case addressed to the Second Person of the Trinity.

Form I is the simpler of the two, and consists of a series of biddings addressed to the congregation, most of them introduced by the word "for" and concluded by a congregational petition addressed to Christ. A form based on this model might begin:

In peace and in faith, let us offer our prayers, saying, "Christ, have mercy."

For peace and tranquility in the world, and for the salvation of all, let us pray.

*Christ, have mercy.*

For N. our Presiding Bishop, for N.(N.) our own Bishop(s), and for all the People of God, let us pray.

*Christ, have mercy.*

Form V consists of a series of petitions addressed directly to Christ, each beginning with "for," but frequently including a result clause beginning with "that." A form based on this model might begin:

We pray to you, O Christ Our God, saying, "Christ, have mercy" (or "Christe eleison").

For the Church of God in every place, that it may persevere in faith and hope, we pray to you.

*Christ, have mercy. (Christe eleison.)*

For all who minister in your Church, (especially _____,) that they may have grace to build up your people in love, we pray to you.

*Christ, have mercy. (Christe eleison.)*

Form IV consists of a series of petitions addressed to the First Person of the Trinity, each followed by an invariable versicle and response which is easily memorized. The following might be used:

God of love and mercy,

*Hear our prayer.*

Forms III and VI are examples of responsive prayer. Unlike the other forms, they require that the complete text be available to all the worshipers. Form VI, when used as a model, also provides an opportunity to compose and use other forms for the Confession of Sin. The rubrics (BCP p. 394) do not require that the Collect that concludes the Prayers be drawn from the Prayer Book. Celebrants and others involved in the planning of liturgy are therefore free to compose new Collects, both for the general use and for the seasons and holy days of the Church Year.

# Confession of Sin

*The Deacon or Celebrant says*

Let us confess our sins to God.

*Silence may be kept.*

*Minister and People*

God of all mercy,
we confess that we have sinned against you,
opposing your will in our lives.
We have denied your goodness in each other,
    in ourselves, and in the world you have created.
We repent of the evil that enslaves us,
    the evil we have done,
    and the evil done on our behalf.
Forgive, restore, and strengthen us
through our Savior Jesus Christ,
that we may abide in your love
and serve only your will. Amen.

# Absolution

Almighty God have mercy on you, forgive you all your sins
through the grace of Jesus Christ, strengthen you in all goodness,
and by the power of the Holy Spirit keep you in eternal life.
*Amen.*

# The Peace

*Celebrant*   The peace of Christ be always with you.
*People*      And also with you.

# Eucharistic Prayer 1

| | |
|---|---|
| *Celebrant* | The Lord be with you. |
| *People* | And also with you. |
| *Celebrant* | Lift up your hearts. |
| *People* | We lift them to the Lord. |
| *Celebrant* | Let us give thanks to the Lord our God. |
| *People* | It is right to give our thanks and praise. |

*Celebrant*　It is truly right, and good and joyful,
to give you thanks, all-holy God,
source of life and fountain of mercy.

*The following Preface may be used at any time.*

You have filled us and all creation with your blessing
and fed us with your constant love;
you have redeemed us in Jesus Christ
and knit us into one body.
Through your Spirit you replenish us
and call us to fullness of life.

*In place of the preceding, a Proper Preface from the Book of Common Prayer
may be used.*

Therefore, joining with Angels and Archangels
and with the faithful of every generation,
we lift our voices with all creation as we sing (say):

*Celebrant and People*

Holy, holy, holy Lord, God of power and might,
heaven and earth are full of your glory.
　Hosanna in the highest.
Blessed is the one who comes in the name of the Lord.
　Hosanna in the highest.

*The Celebrant continues*

Blessed are you, gracious God,
creator of the universe and giver of life.
You formed us in your own image
and called us to dwell in your infinite love.

You gave the world into our care
that we might be your faithful stewards
and show forth your bountiful grace.

But we failed to honor your image
in one another and in ourselves;
we would not see your goodness in the world around us;
and so we violated your creation,
abused one another,
and rejected your love.
Yet you never ceased to care for us,
and prepared the way of salvation for all people.

Through Abraham and Sarah
you called us into covenant with you.
You delivered us from slavery,
sustained us in the wilderness,
and raised up prophets
to renew your promise of salvation.
Then, in the fullness of time,
you sent your eternal Word,
made mortal flesh in Jesus.
Born into the human family,
and dwelling among us,
he revealed your glory.
Giving himself freely to death on the cross,
he triumphed over evil,
opening the way of freedom and life.

*At the following words concerning the bread, the Celebrant is to hold it, or lay a hand upon it; and at the words concerning the cup, to hold or place a hand upon the cup and any other vessel containing wine to be consecrated.*

On the night before he died for us,
Our Savior Jesus Christ took bread,
and when he had given thanks to you,
he broke it, and gave it to his friends, and said:
"Take, eat:
This is my Body which is given for you.
Do this for the remembrance of me."

As supper was ending, Jesus took the cup of wine,
and when he had given thanks,
he gave it to them, and said:
"Drink this, all of you:
This is my Blood of the new Covenant,
which is poured out for you and for all
for the forgiveness of sins.
Whenever you drink it,
do this for the remembrance of me."

Therefore we proclaim the mystery of faith:

*Celebrant and People*

Christ has died.
Christ is risen.
Christ will come again.

*The Celebrant continues*

Remembering his death and resurrection,
we now present to you from your creation
this bread and this wine.
By your Holy Spirit may they be for us
the Body and Blood of our Savior Jesus Christ.
Grant that we who share these gifts
may be filled with the Holy Spirit
and live as Christ's Body in the world.
Bring us into the everlasting heritage
of your daughters and sons,
that with [ _____ and] all your saints,
past, present, and yet to come,
we may praise your Name for ever.

Through Christ and with Christ and in Christ,
in the unity of the Holy Spirit,
to you be honor, glory, and praise,
for ever and ever. *AMEN.*

# Eucharistic Prayer 2

| | |
|---|---|
| *Celebrant* | The Lord be with you. |
| *People* | And also with you. |
| *Celebrant* | Lift up your hearts. |
| *People* | We lift them to the Lord. |
| *Celebrant* | Let us give thanks to the Lord our God. |
| *People* | It is right to give our thanks and praise. |

*Celebrant*

We praise you and we bless you, holy and gracious God,
source of life abundant.
From before time you made ready the creation.
Your Spirit moved over the deep
and brought all things into being:
sun, moon, and stars;
earth, winds, and waters;
and every living thing.
You made us in your image,
and taught us to walk in your ways.
But we rebelled against you, and wandered far away;
and yet, as a mother cares for her children,
you would not forget us.
Time and again you called us
to live in the fullness of your love.

And so this day we join with Saints and Angels
in the chorus of praise that rings through eternity,
lifting our voices to magnify you as we sing (say):

*Celebrant and People*

Holy, holy, holy Lord, God of power and might,
heaven and earth are full of your glory.
  Hosanna in the highest.
Blessed is the one who comes in the name of the Lord.
  Hosanna in the highest.

Glory and honor and praise to you, holy and living God.
To deliver us from the power of sin and death
and to reveal the riches of your grace,
you looked with favor upon Mary, your willing servant,
that she might conceive and bear a son,
Jesus the holy child of God.
Living among us, Jesus loved us.
He broke bread with outcasts and sinners,
healed the sick, and proclaimed good news to the poor.
He yearned to draw all the world to himself
yet we were heedless of his call to walk in love.
Then, the time came for him to complete upon the cross
the sacrifice of his life,
and to be glorified by you.

*At the following words concerning the bread, the Celebrant is to hold it, or lay a hand upon it; and at the words concerning the cup, to hold or place a hand upon the cup and any other vessel containing the wine to be consecrated.*

On the night before he died for us,
Jesus was at table with his friends.
He took bread, gave thanks to you,
broke it, and gave it to them, and said:
"Take, eat:
This is my Body, which is given for you.
Do this for the remembrance of me."
As supper was ending, Jesus took the cup of wine.
Again, he gave thanks to you,
gave it to them, and said:
"Drink this, all of you:
This is my Blood of the new Covenant,
which is poured out for you and for all
for the forgiveness of sins.
Whenever you drink it,
do this for the remembrance of me."

Now gathered at your table, O God of all creation,
and remembering Christ, crucified and risen,
who was and is and is to come,
we offer to you our gifts of bread and wine,
and ourselves, a living sacrifice.

Pour out your Spirit upon these gifts
that they may be the Body and Blood of Christ.
Breathe your Spirit over the whole earth
and make us your new creation,
the Body of Christ given for the world you have made.

In the fullness of time bring us,
with [_____ and] all your saints,
from every tribe and language and people and nation,
to feast at the banquet prepared
from the foundation of the world.

Through Christ and with Christ and in Christ,
in the unity of the Holy Spirit,
to you be honor, glory, and praise,
for ever and ever. *AMEN.*

# Eucharistic Prayer 3

| | |
|---|---|
| *Presider* | The Lord be with you. |
| *People* | And also with you. |
| *Presider* | Lift up your hearts. |
| *People* | We lift them to the Lord. |
| *Presider* | Let us give thanks to the Lord our God. |
| *People* | It is right to give our thanks and praise. |

*Presider*

All thanks and praise
are yours at all times and in all places,
our true and loving God;
through Jesus Christ, your eternal Word,

the Wisdom from on high by whom you created all things.
You laid the foundations of the world
and enclosed the sea when it burst out from the womb;
You brought forth all creatures of the earth
and gave breath to humankind.

Wondrous are you, Holy One of Blessing,
all you create is a sign of hope for our journey;
And so as the morning stars sing your praises
we join the heavenly beings and all creation
as we shout with joy:

*Presider and People*                          *or*

Holy, holy, holy Lord,               Holy, holy, holy Lord,
God of power and might,              God of power and might,
heaven and earth                     heaven and earth
are full of your glory.              are full of your glory.
   Hosanna in the highest.         Hosanna in the highest.
Blessed is the one                   Blessed is he
who comes in the                     who comes in the
name of the Lord.                    name of the Lord.
   Hosanna in the highest.         Hosanna in the highest.

*The Presider continues*

Glory and honor are yours, Creator of all,
your Word has never been silent;
you called a people to yourself, as a light to the nations,
you delivered them from bondage
and led them to a land of promise.
Of your grace, you gave Jesus
to be human, to share our life,
to proclaim the coming of your holy reign
and give himself for us, a fragrant offering.

Through Jesus Christ our Redeemer,
you have freed us from sin,
brought us into your life,
reconciled us to you,
and restored us to the glory you intend for us.

We thank you that on the night before he died for us
Jesus took bread,
and when he had given thanks to you, he broke it,
gave it to his friends and said:
"Take, eat, this is my Body, broken for you.
Do this for the remembrance of me."

After supper Jesus took the cup of wine,
said the blessing, gave it to his friends and said:
"Drink this, all of you:
this cup is the new Covenant in my Blood,
poured out for you and for all
for the forgiveness of sin.
Do this for the remembrance of me."

And so, remembering all that was done for us:
the cross, the tomb, the resurrection and ascension,
longing for Christ's coming in glory,
and presenting to you these gifts
your earth has formed and human hands have made,
we acclaim you, O Christ:

*Presider and People*

Dying, you destroyed our death.
Rising, you restored our life.
Christ Jesus, come in glory!

*The Presider continues*

Send your Holy Spirit upon us
and upon these gifts of bread and wine
that they may be to us
the Body and Blood of your Christ.
Grant that we, burning with your Spirit's power,
may be a people of hope, justice and love.

Giver of Life, draw us together in the Body of Christ,
and in the fullness of time gather us
with [blessed _____, and] all your people
into the joy of our true eternal home.

Through Christ and with Christ and in Christ,
by the inspiration of your Holy Spirit,
we worship you our God and Creator
in voices of unending praise.

*Presider and People*

Blessed are you now and for ever. *AMEN.*

# Forms for the Eucharistic Prayer

*For use with the Order for Celebrating the Holy Eucharist on pages 400–401 of the Book of Common Prayer. In keeping with the rubrics governing the use of the Order, these forms are not intended for use at the principal Sunday or weekly celebration of a congregation.*

## Form A

| | |
|---|---|
| *Celebrant* | The Lord be with you. |
| *People* | And also with you. |
| *Celebrant* | Lift up your hearts. |
| *People* | We lift them to the Lord |
| *Celebrant* | Let us give thanks to the Lord our God. |
| *People* | It is right to give God thanks and praise. |

*The Celebrant gives thanks to God for the created order, and for God's self-revelation to the human race in history;*

*Recalls before God, when appropriate, the particular occasion being celebrated;*

*If desired, incorporates or adapts the Proper Preface of the Day.*

> *If the Sanctus is to be included, it is introduced with these or similar words*

And so we join the saints and angels in proclaiming your glory, as we sing (say),

*Celebrant and People*

Holy, holy, holy Lord, God of power and might,
heaven and earth are full of your glory.
   Hosanna in the highest.
Blessed is the one who comes in the name of the Lord.
   Hosanna in the highest.

*The Celebrant now praises God for the salvation of the world through Christ Jesus.*

*The Prayer continues with these words*

And so, we offer you these gifts.
Sanctify them by your Holy Spirit
to be for your people the Body and Blood of Christ.

*At the following words concerning the bread, the Celebrant is to hold it, or lay a hand upon it; and at the words concerning the cup, to hold or place a hand upon the cup and any other vessel containing wine to be consecrated.*

On the night before he died for us,
our Savior Jesus Christ took bread,
and when he had given thanks to you,
he broke it, and gave it to his friends, and said:
"Take, eat:
This is my Body which is given for you.
Do this for the remembrance of me."

As supper was ending, Jesus took the cup of wine,
and when he had given thanks,
he gave it to them, and said:
"Drink this, all of you:
This is my blood of the new Covenant,
which is poured out for you and for all
for the forgiveness of sins.
Whenever you drink it,
do this for the remembrance of me."

*The Celebrant may then introduce, with suitable words, a memorial acclamation by the people.*

*The Celebrant then continues*

We now celebrate, O God, the memorial of Christ our Savior.
By means of this holy bread and cup,
we show forth the sacrifice of Christ's death,
and proclaim the resurrection,
until Christ comes in glory.

Gather us by this Holy Communion
into one body in the Risen One,
and make us a living sacrifice of praise.
Through Christ and with Christ and in Christ,
in the unity of the Holy Spirit,
to you be honor, glory, and praise,
for ever and ever. *AMEN.*

## Form B

| | |
|---|---|
| *Celebrant* | The Lord be with you. |
| *People* | And also with you. |
| *Celebrant* | Lift up your hearts. |
| *People* | We lift them to the Lord. |
| *Celebrant* | Let us give thanks to the Lord our God. |
| *People* | It is right to give God thanks and praise. |

*The Celebrant gives thanks to God for the created order, and for God's self-revelation to the human race in history;*

*Recalls before God, when appropriate, the particular occasion being celebrated;*

*If desired, incorporates or adapts the Proper Preface of the Day.*

*If the Sanctus is to be included, it is introduced with these or similar words*

And so we join the saints and angels in proclaiming your glory, as we sing (say),

*Celebrant and People*

Holy, holy, holy Lord, God of power and might,
heaven and earth are full of your glory.
    Hosanna in the highest.
Blessed is the one who comes in the name of the Lord.
    Hosanna in the highest.

*The Celebrant now praises God for the salvation of the world through Christ Jesus.*

*At the following words concerning the bread, the Celebrant is to hold it, or lay a hand upon it; and at the words concerning the cup, to hold or place a hand upon the cup and any other vessel containing wine to be consecrated.*

On the night before he died for us,
our Savior Jesus Christ took bread,
and when he had given thanks to you,
he broke it, and gave it to his friends, and said:
"Take, eat:
This is my Body which is given for you.
Do this for the remembrance of me."

As supper was ending, Jesus took the cup of wine,
and when he had given thanks,
he gave it to them, and said:
"Drink this, all of you:
This is my blood of the new Covenant,
which is poured out for you and for all
for the forgiveness of sins.
Whenever you drink it,
do this for the remembrance of me."

*The Celebrant may then introduce, with suitable words, a memorial acclamation by the people.*

*The Celebrant then continues*

Remembering now the suffering and death
and proclaiming the resurrection and ascension
of Jesus our Redeemer,
we bring before you these gifts.
Sanctify them by your Holy Spirit
to be for your people the Body and Blood of Christ.

*The Celebrant then prays that all may receive the benefits of Christ's work, and the renewal of the Holy Spirit.*

*The Prayer concludes with these or similar words*

Through Christ and with Christ and in Christ,
in the unity of the Holy Spirit,
to you be honor, glory, and praise,
for ever and ever. *AMEN.*

# Fraction Anthems

*Any of the following, or a Fraction Anthem from The Hymnal 1982, S167–S172, may be said or sung in place of the anthem "Christ our Passover" (BCP, p. 364).*

We break this bread
to share in the Body of Christ.
*We who are many are one body,*
*for we all share in the one bread.*

God of promise, you have prepared a banquet for us.
*Happy are those who are called to the Supper of the Lamb.*

This is the true bread which comes down from heaven and gives
life to the world.
*Whoever eats this bread will live for ever.*

Lamb of God, you take away the sins of the world:
    have mercy on us.
Lamb of God, you take away the sins of the world:
    have mercy on us.
Lamb of God, you take away the sins of the world:
    grant us peace.

# Postcommunion Prayer

God of abundance,
you have fed us
with the bread of life and cup of salvation;
you have united us
with Christ and one another;
and you have made us one
with all your people in heaven and on earth.
Now send us forth
in the power of your Spirit,
that we may proclaim your redeeming love to the world
and continue for ever
in the risen life of Christ our Savior. Amen.

*or*

Loving God,
we give you thanks
for restoring us in your image
and nourishing us with spiritual food
in the Sacrament of Christ's Body and Blood.
Now send us forth
a people, forgiven, healed, renewed;
that we may proclaim your love to the world
and continue in the risen life of Christ our Savior. Amen.

# Blessings

Holy eternal Majesty,
Holy incarnate Word,
Holy abiding Spirit,
Bless you for evermore. *Amen.*

May the blessing of the God of Abraham and Sarah, and of Jesus
Christ born of our sister Mary, and of the Holy Spirit, who broods
over the world as a mother over her children, be upon you and
remain with you always. *Amen.*

God's Blessing be with you,
Christ's peace be with you,
the Spirit's outpouring be with you,
now and always. *Amen.*
(source: Celtic)

The Wisdom of God
the Love of God
and the Grace of God
strengthen you
to be Christ's hands and heart in this world,
in the name of the Holy Trinity. *Amen.*
(source: Celtic)

Live without fear: your Creator has made you holy, has always
protected you, and loves you as a mother. Go in peace to follow
the good road and may God's blessing be with you always. *Amen.*
(source: from Saint Clare)

# Notes

P. 20 The morning versicle is drawn from Psalm 71:8. In medieval offices it was part of the suffrages at Prime. The evening versicle is from Psalm 71:12.

P. 20 This doxology focuses on the unity of the Triune God. It is similar to the opening doxology of Byzantine Vespers, which reads, "Glory to the holy, consubstantial, lifegiving and undivided Trinity: always, now and ever, and to ages of ages." The opening words "Praise to" distinguish it from other forms.

Pp. 20-21 The translation of the second half of these antiphons, "O come let us worship," is taken from the Canadian *Book of Alternative Services*. The Latin original, "Venite adoremus," contains no pronoun specifying the object of worship; hence the translation is a more literal translation of the original text while still providing the number of syllables required for Anglican chant.

P. 21 The alternative Lenten antiphon "Today..." is derived from the text of Psalm 95.

P. 21 The antiphon for Trinity Sunday is similar to the medieval Latin antiphon, "The true God, One in Trinity and Trinity in Unity, O come let us worship," appointed for Trinity Sunday.

P. 21 This text of Psalm 95 has been revised to use direct address to God, in a manner similar to The Song of Zechariah and The Song of Mary prepared by the English Language Liturgical Consultation (see below, Canticles 15 and 16).

P. 22 Psalm 63 is a traditional morning psalm used in many ancient forms of the morning office. It appears as an alternative to *Venite* or *Jubilate* in the Canadian *Book of Alternative Services*.

P. 23 Psalm 67 is provided as a morning psalm in the new Roman Catholic *Liturgy of the Hours*.

P. 23 "Light of the World," metrical paraphrase of the *Phos hilaron*, © Paul Gibson.

P. 24 Psalm 134 is a traditional evening psalm used as an invitatory in the *Alternative Service Book* of the Church of England and in the Canadian *Book of Alternative Services*.

P. 24 Psalm 141 is the opening psalm in the oldest known forms of the evening office. It occupies this same position in the *Lutheran Book of Worship* and in a number of other modern service books.

P. 24 Antiphon on Psalm 63. This text is the traditional antiphon, and derives from the Greek version of the first verse of the psalm, which specifically mentions daybreak.

P. 24 Antiphon on Psalm 67. The first antiphon is taken from the psalm itself. The alternative antiphon is from Psalm 145:2.

P. 24 Antiphon on Psalm 134. The text is from Psalm 74:15, which is also appointed as an opening sentence at Evening Prayer (BCP p. 115).

P. 24 Antiphon on Psalm 141. This text is a traditional antiphon and is drawn from the psalm itself. It is also appointed as an opening sentence at Evening Prayer (BCP p.115).

P. 25 The suggestion that the texts of the seasonal opening sentences might be used as antiphons is also derived from the Prayer Book (p. 141).

P. 27 Two changes have been made in the translation of the Magnificat recommended by ELLC. The first is in lines 2 and 3, where the ELLC text reads "my spirit rejoices in God my Savior, for you, Lord, have looked with favor . . ." It seemed to the commission more felicitous to establish the fact of direct address in the second line.

The other is in lines 15 and 16 where the ELLC version reads ". . . to the aid of your servant Israel, to remember the promise of mercy." The commission preferred "help" to "aid," and found line 16 awkward.

P. 30 Canticle A. This is a translation from the original Greek of a text which is also included as a canticle in the Canadian *Book of Alternative Services.* Musical settings for this canticle can be found in *Wonder, Love, and Praise* (a supplement to *The Hymnal 1982*) 904 and 905.

P. 30 Canticle B. This canticle is from the Mozarabic (medieval Spanish) Psalter and is a new translation from the Latin. For a musical setting see *Wonder, Love, and Praise* 906.

P. 42 Alternative to salutation. The use of a supplicatory verse in place of "The Lord be with you" and its reply was common in medieval forms of the office. See BCP Noonday and Compline for examples of this usage. This text is drawn from Psalm 61:1.

P. 42 Sources for the Suffrages are Psalms 79:9, 74:2, 29:11b, 96:3, 74:20a, 74:18b, 36:10, 90:14.

P. 53 The Nicene Creed. The 1994 General Convention affirmed the following resolutions:

*Resolved*, the House of Deputies concurring, **That this 71st General Convention, following the resolution of the 68th General Convention, and responding to Resolution 19 of the joint meeting of the Primates of the Anglican Communion and the Anglican Consultative Council (Capetown 1993), hereby reaffirm its intention to remove the words "and the Son" from the third paragraph of the Nicene Creed at the next revision of the Book of Common Prayer.**

*Resolved*, the House of Bishops concurring, **That this 71st General Convention direct that when the English Language**

Liturgical Consultation (ELLC) text of the Nicene Creed (included in *Supplemental Liturgical Materials*) is used, the words "and the Son" be omitted, such use always to be under the direction of the diocesan bishop or ecclesiastical authority, and with an appropriate educational component.

The following background material provides the historical rationale for this decision, and provides material to be included in educational events.

The original wording of the Nicene Creed, "I believe in the Holy Spirit, who proceeds from the Father, who with the Father and the Son is worshiped and glorified," was agreed upon at the fourth-century Ecumenical Council of Constantinople (Ecumenical Councils are councils of bishops and theologians of the entire Church). The wording was altered in the Latin half of the Church by the addition of the words, "who proceeds from the Father *and the Son*," a change expressed in Latin by one word: *filioque*. This addition was made at a sixth-century regional synod meeting in Toledo, Spain. In this region many Christians had originally been Arians who denied the full divinity of the Son. The synod apparently believed that the constant liturgical repetition of the *filioque* clause would aid in teaching the faithful that the Son was fully God. The phrase gradually spread until, by the eleventh century, it was in general use in the Latin Church. Its inclusion has never been authorized by an Ecumenical Council and has never been adopted by the Eastern churches.

In the sixteenth and seventeenth centuries, Anglican theologians were unanimous in claiming that the only true bases of doctrine were Scripture and the teaching of the undivided Church (i.e., the five Ecumenical Councils held between the years 325 and 451). The Church of England taught only what Scripture and tradition taught, they asserted. Not knowing the full history of the *filioque* addition and mistakenly assuming that it had always formed part of the Creed, Anglicans retained the phrase, and some divines even went to great lengths to explain why the Greeks deleted it!

The continued use of the *filioque* phrase by churches in the West remains a source of irritation between East and West. The unilateral altering of a Creed originally authorized by an Ecumenical Council strikes Eastern Orthodox Christians as ecclesiologically high-handed and canonically indefensible. The theology of the Holy Spirit which has grown up in the West since the introduction of the *filioque* is a point of serious, but less-heated, misunderstanding between East and West.

In 1976, the Anglican members of the Anglican-Orthodox Joint Doctrinal Commission said in an Agreed Statement that the *filioque* should not be included in the Creed because it had been introduced without the authority of an Ecumenical Council. In 1978 Anglican bishops meetings at the Lambeth Conference recommended that churches of the Anglican Communion consider omitting the *filioque* from the Nicene Creed. The 1985 General Convention recommended the restoration of the original wording of the Creed, once this action had been approved by the Lambeth Conference and the Anglican Consultative Council. The change was then endorsed by the Lambeth Conference of 1988, the 1990 meeting of the Anglican Consultative Council, and the 1993 joint meeting of Anglican Primates and the Anglican Consultative Council. The 1994 General Convention affirmed the intention of the Episcopal Church to remove the *filioque* clause at the next revision of the Book of Common Prayer.

Whether or not to restore the original wording of the Nicene Creed is not primarily a theological issue. The relation of the Holy Spirit to the first and second persons of the Holy Trinity remains a matter of theological discussion and is ultimately unknowable, at least on this side of the grave. The real issue is twofold:

1. on what authority a statement of faith agreed upon by bishops and theologians of the whole Church, East and West, may be changed; and

2. what course is most faithful to the theological traditions of Anglicanism. A good introduction to the issues, suitable for parish study, is found in Marianne H. Micks, *Loving the Questions: An Exploration of the Nicene Creed* (Cowley Publications, 1993).

—*The Rev. Dr. Ruth Meyers*

P. 57 Eucharistic Prayer 1. The use of "all" ("My Blood...poured out for you and for all") in the institution narrative emphasizes that forgiveness of sins is made available to all through Christ's sacrifice. While the Greek word is literally translated "many," biblical scholars have pointed out that in the context of the passage it means that the sacrifice is made not just for a large number of persons, but for all humanity. (A similar use of "many" occurs in Matthew 20:28, where it is written that Jesus would give his life as "a ransom for many." 1 Timothy 2:6, looking back on the event, says he gave himself as a "ransom for all.") New eucharistic prayers in both the Roman Catholic Church and the Lutheran Church use "all" rather than "many."

P. 62 Eucharistic Prayer 3. The underlying pattern of this eucharistic prayer is thanksgiving and supplication. Thomas Talley, Professor Emeritus of the General Theological Seminary, has argued that this basic structure underlies the diversity of classical eucharistic prayers in both the eastern and western liturgical traditions prior to the Reformation (see Prof. Talley's article, "The Structure of the Eucharistic Prayer," in *A Prayer Book for the Twenty-first Century*, Liturgical Studies 3 [Church Hymnal Corporation, 1996], pp. 76-101; see also the findings of the fifth international Anglican Liturgical Consultation, which met in Dublin, Ireland, in August 1995: David R. Holeton (ed.), *Renewing the Anglican Eucharist* [Grove Books, 1996], pp. 25-27).

In this classic pattern of eucharistic prayer, praise to the Creator leads into the *Sanctus*. This is followed by thanksgiving for redemption, climaxing in the narrative of the institution and leading into a memorial oblation, that is, remembering the passion, death and resurrection of Jesus and offering gifts of bread and wine. Following this oblation, the prayer shifts to supplication, with an invocation of the Holy Spirit upon the bread and wine and upon the gathered community.

To underscore that the institution narrative is part of the thanksgiving for redemption, this eucharistic prayer introduces the institution narrative with the words "We thank you." To strengthen the unity of the thanksgiving for redemption and the memorial oblation, an acclamation by the people follows the oblation and leads into the supplication.

The text of the opening dialogue (*sursum corda*) is that of the English Language Liturgical Consultation (ELLC), which consists of representatives of major English-speaking churches throughout the world. The final line, "It is right to give our thanks and praise," renders a Latin and Greek text which is literally translated "It is right and just," a wording that seems rather curt in English. "To give our thanks" was chosen as a reflection of "Let us give our thanks" in the previous line; the context makes clear that the thanks and praise are being given to God. The ELLC text has been widely adopted by Anglican churches as well as in other denominations.

Two alternatives are provided for the *Sanctus*. "Blessed is the one who comes in the name of the Lord" follows the New Revised Standard Version of the Bible in translating Psalm 118:26 and Matthew 21:9 (and the parallel texts, Mark 11:9 and John 12:13) as "Blessed is the one." However, in the context of the eucharistic prayer the quotation refers specifically to Jesus our Savior and not to everyone who comes in God's name. For this reason the ELLC text reads "Blessed is he."

The language of the preface is derived from Job 38:4-11 and Wisdom of Solomon 9:1-2. The identification of Jesus as eternal Word and Wisdom, while not widely known in the late twentieth century, is evident in the New Testament and the writings of the early Church. During the inter-testamental period (the second and first centuries B.C.E.), personified Wisdom came to be understood as a manifestation of God, an agent of creation and salvation. Some New Testament scholars argue that early Christians interpreted Jesus' life, death and resurrection in light of the already familiar language and ideas of divine Wisdom. The third-century writers Origen and Tertullian identified Jesus as Wisdom, and two centuries later Augustine of Hippo, in a treatise on the Holy Trinity, named Jesus as Word and Wisdom.

The phrase "Holy One of Blessing" originated in a Jewish congregation as a contemporary reformulation of the traditional Jewish invocation "Blessed are you, Lord our God, King of the universe."

Pp. 65-68  Forms for the Eucharistic Prayer. These forms are modeled on Forms 1 and 2 on pages 402-405 of the Book of Common Prayer. Following the Prayer Book, Form 1 places the invocation of the Holy Spirit before the words of institution, and Form 2 places it after them.

The texts of the opening dialogue, Sanctus, and concluding doxology are identical with those in two complete eucharistic prayers (see pages 57-62). The institution narrative is the same as in Eucharistic Prayer 1.

P. 70  The Seventy-second General Convention passed the following version of the first Celtic blessing, which had been altered in committee: "The blessing of God be with you, the peace of Christ be in you, the outpouring of the Spirit be upon you now and always." A number of theologians found this open to a modalist construction. Since the changes had been made for purely literary reasons, the original version has been restored.

# Opening Acclamation

*Celebrant*

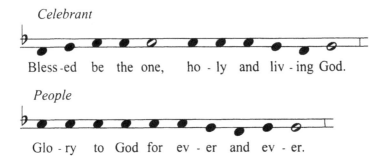

Bless -ed be the one, ho - ly and liv - ing God.

*People*

Glo - ry to God for ev - er and ev - er.

# Opening Acclamation

*Celebrant*

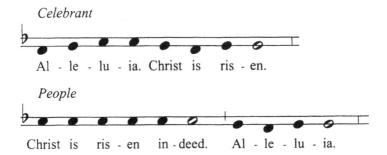

Al - le - lu - ia. Christ is ris - en.

*People*

Christ is ris - en in - deed. Al - le - lu - ia.

# Opening Acclamation

*Celebrant*

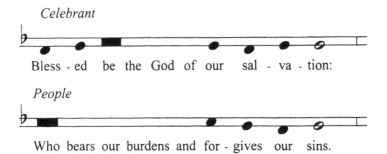

Bless - ed be the God of our sal - va - tion:

*People*

Who bears our burdens and for - gives our sins.

# Eucharist Prayer 1   Preface

It is truly right, and good and joy - ful, to give you thanks,

all - ho - ly God, source of life and foun - tain of mer - cy.

You have filled us and all creation with your blessing and fed

us with your con - stant love; you have redeemed us in

Jesus Christ and knit us in - to one bo - dy. Through your Spir - it

you re - plen - ish us and call us to full - ness of life.

There - fore, join - ing with An - gels and Arch - an - gels

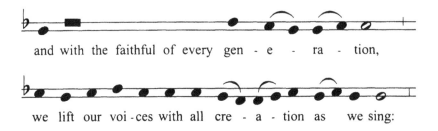

and with the faithful of every gen - e - ra - tion,

we lift our voi - ces with all cre - a - tion as we sing:

# Eucharistic Prayer 1 Concluding Doxology

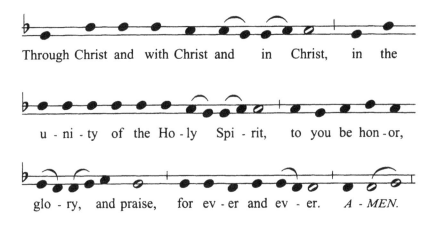

Through Christ and with Christ and in Christ, in the

u - ni - ty of the Ho - ly Spi - rit, to you be hon - or,

glo - ry, and praise, for ev - er and ev - er. *A - MEN.*

Chant adaptation by Bruce E. Ford, 1992.

# Eucharistic Prayer 2   Preface

We praise you and we   bless you,   ho - ly  and gra-cious God,

source of    life    a - bun - dant.  From be-fore time you made

ready the cre  -  a  -  tion.   Your Spirit  moved  over  the  deep

and brought all things in - to   be - ing:  sun,  moon,  and  stars;

earth, winds, and   wa - ters;    and    ev - 'ry  liv - ing thing.

You made us in your  im - age,    and   taught    us   to    walk

in  your ways. But we  rebelled  against  you,  and

wan-dered   far    a - way;    and yet, as a mother cares for her

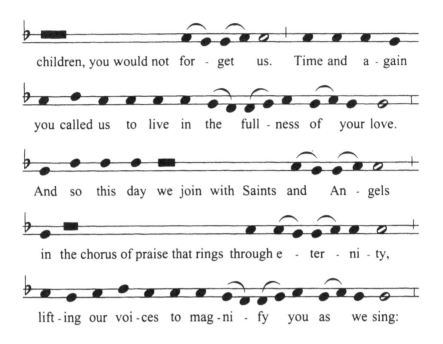

children, you would not for - get us. Time and a - gain

you called us to live in the full - ness of your love.

And so this day we join with Saints and An - gels

in the chorus of praise that rings through e - ter - ni - ty,

lift - ing our voi - ces to mag - ni - fy you as we sing:

## Eucharistic Prayer 2   Concluding Doxology

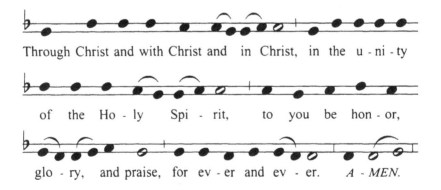

Through Christ and with Christ and in Christ, in the u - ni - ty

of the Ho - ly Spi - rit, to you be hon - or,

glo - ry, and praise, for ev - er and ev - er. *A - MEN.*

# Eucharistic Prayer 3 Preface

All thanks and praise are yours at all times and in all pla - ces,

our true and lov - ing God; through Je - sus Christ, your

e - ter - nal Word, the Wis - dom from on high by whom you

cre - at - ed all things. You laid the foun - da - tions

of the world and en - closed the sea when it burst out of

the womb; You brought forth all crea - tures of the earth

and gave breath to hu - man-kind. Won - drous are you,

Ho - ly One of Bless - ing, all you cre - ate is a sign

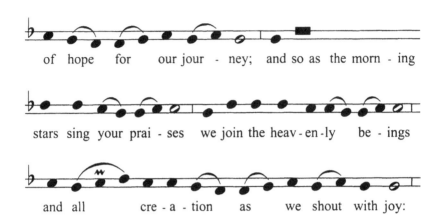

of hope for our jour - ney; and so as the morn - ing

stars sing your prai - ses we join the heav - en -ly be - ings

and all cre - a - tion as we shout with joy:

# Eucharistic Prayer 3  Concluding Doxology

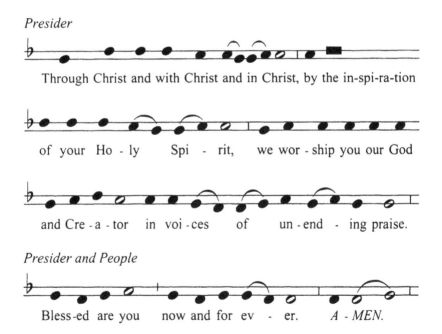

*Presider*

Through Christ and with Christ and in Christ, by the in-spi-ra-tion

of your Ho - ly Spi - rit, we wor - ship you our God

and Cre - a - tor in voi -ces of un - end - ing praise.

*Presider and People*

Bless -ed are you now and for ev - er. *A - MEN.*

# Fraction Anthem

*Cantor*

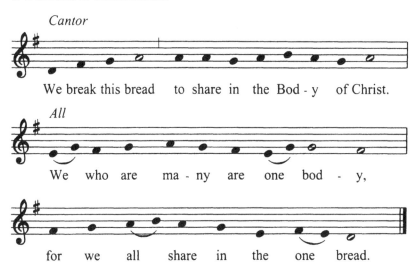

We break this bread    to share in  the Bod - y    of Christ.

*All*

We   who   are     ma - ny    are     one    bod   -   y,

for    we    all     share    in    the    one    bread.

Centonized Mode 7 antiphon melody by Bruce E. Ford, 1992.


# Fraction Anthem

*Cantor*

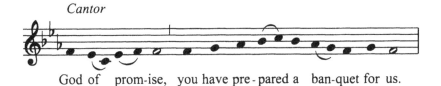

God of    prom-ise,  you have pre - pared a    ban-quet for us.

*All*

Hap-py are those who are called to the Sup-per of the Lamb.

Centonized Mode 2 melody by Bruce E. Ford, 1992.

# Fraction Anthem

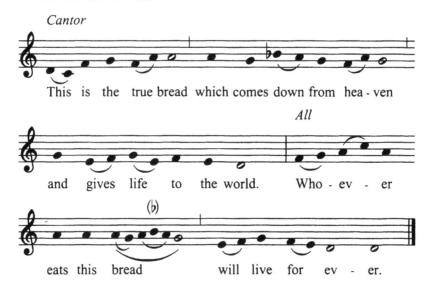

*Cantor*

This is the true bread which comes down from hea - ven

*All*

and gives life to the world. Who - ev - er

eats this bread will live for ev - er.

Centonized Mode 1 melody by Bruce E. Ford, 1992.